A poster of Chung Ling Soo performing Botania, the production of a flower bush from a large cone.

Magic and Illusion

Michael Symes

A Shire book

Published in 2004 by Shire Publications Ltd,
Cromwell House, Church Street, Princes Risborough,
Buckinghamshire HP27 9AA, UK.
(Website: www.shirebooks.co.uk)

Copyright © 2004 by Michael Symes.
First published 2004.
Shire Album 433. ISBN 0 7478 0604 7.
Michael Symes is hereby identified as the author of this
work in accordance with Section 77 of the Copyright,
Designs and Patents Act 1988.

British Library Cataloguing in Publication Data:
Symes, Michael
Magic and illusion. – (Shire album; 433)
1. Magic tricks – History
2. Magicians – History
I. Title
793.8'09
ISBN 0 7478 0604 7.

Cover: *A poster of the magician Ionia, c.1910, and the Cups and Balls used by Prince Charles at The Magic Circle in 1975.*

ACKNOWLEDGEMENTS
Photographs are acknowledged as follows: Davenports, page 15 (bottom two); Cadbury
Lamb, page 39; from The Magic Circle collections, pages 1, 3, 4, 5, 6 (both), 7, 8, 9, 10
(both), 11 (all), 13 (all), 14 (bottom), 15 (top), 16 (top right and bottom), 17 (bottom left),
18 (top right and bottom), 19 (both), 20 (all), 21 (all), 22 (both), 23 (all), 24 (all), 25 (all), 26
(all), 33, 34 (all), 35 (all), 36 (all), 38 (bottom), front cover (both); from Michael Symes's
collection, pages 14 (top), 16 (top left), 27, 28 (all), 29 (both), 30, 31, 32 (all); John A.
Thompson, pages 17 (top and bottom right), 18 (top left), 37, 38 (top). Original
photography by David A. Ross, LRPS. Special thanks are due to The Magic Circle for
their co-operation in providing so many illustrations and objects for illustration. The
author is particularly indebted to John Fisher, Executive Curator of the Museum of The
Magic Circle.

Printed in Malta by Gutenberg Press Limited, Gudja Road,
Tarxien PLA 19, Malta

Contents

A brief survey of magic 4

Some performers and their acts 9

Magical apparatus 19

Dealers and makers 27

Magic posters 33

Magicians' societies 37

Further reading 39

Index 40

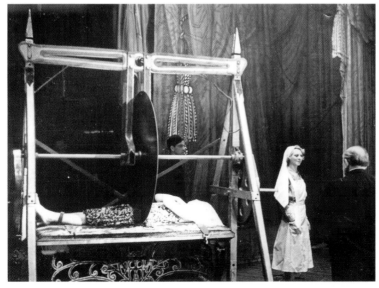

Horace Goldin, an international performer of the first half of the twentieth century, performs the horrifying buzz-saw illusion, apparently slicing an assistant in two.

A brief survey of magic

Magic as entertainment has an extremely long history, dating at least as far back as to the ancient Egyptians. The magician Dedi, summoned to the court of King Cheops in 2600 BC, performed such wonders as decapitating fowl and other creatures and restoring them to life. The oldest classic trick in the modern repertoire, the Cups and Balls, was well established by the time of the Romans and is described in accounts by Seneca and other writers. From the Middle Ages the performance of magic was sometimes confused with witchcraft, and indeed the terms 'magician' and 'conjurer' had connotations of the black arts whereas magical entertainers were known as 'jugglers'. It was not much before 1800 that magic as we know it today was fully accepted in the West purely as a form of entertainment free from any association with witchcraft.

In this book we shall be concerned with magic since 1800. During the nineteenth century three developments laid the foundations for magic in its modern form: the rise of stage magic, the growth in popularity of magic in the Victorian parlour and the adoption of magic as a hobby. The stage in general was often seen as an immoral place but as the century wore on it became increasingly respectable, as evidenced by the popularity of Gilbert and Sullivan, whose operettas were considered suitable family entertainment. This respectability extended to magic, and the partnership of Maskelyne and Cooke (later Maskelyne and Devant) at the Egyptian Hall,

Jasper Maskelyne, of the Maskelyne dynasty of performers, produces cannon-balls from nowhere.

*A bronze bust of David Devant by Faith Winter,
with a poster of the great magician behind.*

Piccadilly, and then at St George's Hall, Langham Place, in London, provided fare for all ages and all classes.

In the middle-class Victorian home the parlour gained in importance. Here the family gathered round the piano to sing ballads and began to invite in hired professional performers, especially magicians. This gave rise to performers known as society entertainers, who would perform at events ranging from well-to-do children's birthday parties to royal gatherings. The Victorians were accomplished at making their own entertainment and, in this spirit, the amateur magician came into his own. Many well-known Victorians, including Dickens, Disraeli, Brunel, W. S. Gilbert and Lewis Carroll, performed magic as a hobby and magical dealers flourished accordingly.

The mid-nineteenth-century performer tended to retain the image of the old wizard, wearing long robes and with tables piled high with ponderous apparatus. We will see in the next chapter how Robert-Houdin changed all that, with his elegant evening dress and simple stage set. The magician was beginning to change from someone claiming to have supernatural powers to a modern entertainer. The importance of publicity was also recognised at this time: John Henry Anderson, the Wizard of the North, had his name on pavements and even on the pats of butter served in the local hotels.

At the beginning of the twentieth century magic comprised both large-scale stage shows, often touring with a company of assistants,

Left: *Max Sterling, who was famed in the early twentieth century for his Japanese-style act with the minimum of props.*

Below: *Howard Thurston, the celebrated American magician, performs the Iasis illusion, vanishing an assistant from a suspended cabinet.*

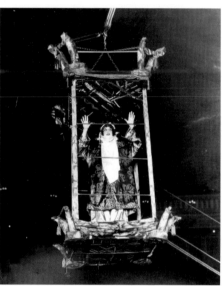

and also more compact, simple acts. Specialists arose, such as Nelson Downs, whose act consisted almost entirely of coins, George Stillwell, who came on to a stage bare except for a T-stand and left it covered with coloured silk handkerchiefs, Howard Thurston, among others, who performed with a pack of cards, and Max Sterling, whose principal props were a sheet of paper, a glass and a fan.

Several movements and trends in magic appeared in the twentieth century, along with a diversity of types of magic. Magic can be divided into a number of distinct categories – close-up, stage, illusions, manipulation, cabaret, street magic, mentalism, children's and stand-up – and many performers specialised in one or more rather than encompass them all. In addition, there are related arts such as ventriloquism, fire-eating, balloon-modelling and juggling, any of which might form part of a magician's repertoire. Escapology, the art of escaping from restraints, was made famous by Houdini (though the term was actually coined by Murray, a successor to Houdini). Again, some performers specialised in escapes, while others might incorporate one such item within a programme of magic. In the case of the Thumb Tie, a feat supposedly of Japanese origin and a variant of escapology, the thumbs are tied but objects such as hoops or chair backs are passed on to the performer's arms and pulled off again. 'Illusions' means large magic with a human assistant, who may be subjected to some form of mutilation, such as

Murray, an Australian magician and escapologist, prepares to perform the fearsome Guillotine illusion.

being sawn in half, divided into small segments or impaled on a sword. 'Manipulation' refers to sleight-of-hand magic – producing cards or coins from thin air, for example. 'Mentalism' covers the various elements of magic of the mind, such as predicting what will happen, conveying thoughts telepathically or reading someone's mind. 'Close-up' has gone through a number of changes: once referred to as 'pocket tricks', it can now be 'table-hopping' (moving from table to table at a restaurant) or 'strolling magician' (mingling with guests at a reception). 'Cabaret', or after-dinner or nightclub magic, was very popular after the Second World War but since then has somewhat declined.

Just as the types of magic differ widely, so do the types of magician. Today, society entertainers have been replaced by corporate entertainers who perform at functions arranged by a firm or company. Magicians who work for a company for publicity or marketing purposes are known as trade show performers. There are magicians who tailor their work to television and the scope that that medium affords.

Magic can be presented through the spoken word (patter) or in silence to music. Manipulation is almost always performed silently, and much stage illusion can likewise be delivered wordlessly as the effect is visual and can be followed without a commentary. The performer always needs to project his or her personality, however, in whatever way connects best with the audience. Before 1900 magic was hardly ever silent but the considerations of performing globally have since made it an attractive option.

*Chefalo, a popular performer of the first
half of the twentieth century, with the cards
that rise from the pack on command.*

Venues have also changed. Music halls for many years provided
the opportunity for a performer to present a single act on the circuit
and never need to change it. After the Second World War the death
of music hall meant that many performers had to expand their
repertoire. On the other hand new opportunities have arisen, such as
television or working on cruise liners, where over two or three weeks
a magician might be expected to perform anything up to half-a-
dozen acts. Despite the changes, the magic routines that have
become classics, the Cups and Balls, Chinese Rings, Egg Bag, Find
the Lady and Four-Ace Trick, are alive and well and likely to
continue to be performed by many magicians for a long time to
come.

Some performers and their acts

It is often said that the performer is more important than his or her tricks, and magic has produced an impressive line of colourful characters, lively personalities and consummate showmen. We shall begin with Jean Eugène Robert-Houdin (1805–71), often called the 'Father of Modern Magic'. This Frenchman was the first recognisably modern performer. The ingenuity of his intricate automata and mechanical devices, such as an orange tree that bore fruit and a pastry cook producing whatever refreshments the audience ordered, put him ahead of his contemporaries. He also insisted on a simple stage setting with the minimum of props, an emphasis on sleight-of-hand and the wearing of smart, contemporary evening dress. The magician's trademark 'top hat and tails' dates from Robert-Houdin. Among the contemporaries who were influenced by him was the Viennese salon entertainer Johann Hofzinser (1806–75), who was famed for his work with cards and his poetical creations such as a mirror in which a rose appeared, changed colour and vanished.

In the United States Harry Kellar (1849–1922) was the first of many famous magicians. He performed worldwide, learning many languages in the process, and concentrated on large-scale effects and illusions, prominent among which was his levitation (floating) of a woman. His great rival was Alexander Herrmann (1844–96), one of a dynasty of magical Herrmanns stretching before and since, including his daughter Adelaide. Herrmann and Kellar used to race each other to engagements in various parts of the world and attack each other in print; they even exposed each other's tricks on occasion. A man who had acted as assistant to both was William Ellsworth Robinson (1861–1918), who set up on his own account, initially in response to a genuine oriental performer, Ching Ling Foo, as 'Chung Ling Soo, Marvellous Chinese Conjurer'. He maintained the illusion of being Chinese so perfectly, speaking to the public through an interpreter, that many never suspected his true origin. Soo developed an immensely successful act of Chinese magic,

Alexander Herrmann, an American stage performer in the late nineteenth century.

including the Linking Rings, Aerial Fishing and illusions such as the Birth of a Pearl, the appearance of a young lady from a shell. One of the effects that most impressed his audience was the bullet-catching feat, which went tragically wrong at the Wood Green Empire theatre in London on 23rd March 1918 through a mechanical defect in the rifle used.

Kellar named as his own successor a card manipulator called Howard Thurston (1869–1936). He progressed to a full evening show in which his card work was integrated into a general programme of illusions and large effects, eventually assisted by his daughter Jane, who had her own solo spot. Contemporary with Thurston was the man who is probably more famous than any other magician – Harry Houdini (1874–1926). Born Ehrich Weiss in Hungary, he came to the United States early on and started as a conventional conjurer, specialising in cards. His stage name came from Robert-Houdin, whom at one time he revered, though not

later. While struggling to make money on a European tour Houdini developed his escapology routines – and also his flair for publicity. The greatest showman since John Henry Anderson, he challenged and defied allcomers to straitjacket, shackle and confine him in various dangerous ways, and his exploits became famous throughout the world. He could escape from a packing case underwater and also from a glass tank of water, upside down. Although his name is synonymous with

Left: *Howard Thurston goes Aerial Fishing, catching goldfish from the air.*

Right: *Howard Thurston turns his entire company into human water fountains.*

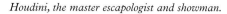

Houdini, the master escapologist and showman.

escapology, he continued to perform general magic, and his full evening show in the 1920s consisted of a mixture of magic and an exposé of the methods used by fraudulent mediums, about which he was passionate.

In contrast to the flamboyant, publicity-hungry Houdini, a quieter showman was Karl Germain (1878–1959). In his relatively brief career, cut short by blindness, he developed a truly original and artistic approach to the creation of magic: butterflies of silk would appear, a whole rosebush, complete with real roses, grow from nothing, a gong vanish when struck, and five empty metal jars fill up with water. In addition to his own inventions he brought to his magic a charming presentation and fanciful patter.

Karl Germain, an artistic performer and creator from the early years of the twentieth century.

The genial Harry Blackstone (1885–1965) succeeded Thurston as the foremost entertainer of his day. His varied act included a girl being produced and then vanished from a stack of car tyres, a vanishing birdcage, a borrowed handkerchief that danced by itself and, most famously, an illuminated light bulb that floated around the stage before veering out over the heads of the audience. Much of the repertoire, including the floating light bulb, was performed with great distinction by his son, Harry Blackstone Junior (1934–97). Meanwhile, the legendary manipulator Cardini (Richard Pitchford, 1895–1973) worked entirely with sleight-of-hand, creating what many have

Harry Blackstone Senior, the doyen of American magicians in the mid twentieth century.

considered to be the greatest act of its kind. Born in Wales, he settled
in the United States and developed an act that was as much about
character-acting as skill, playing a slightly tipsy man-about-town to
whom magical things happened by surprise.

Joseph Dunninger (1892–1975) moved on from a general act in
the 1930s that included items such as the Egg Bag and Linking
Rings as well as mind-reading to concentrate on the latter, becoming
the leading mentalist of his day and working until the 1960s. His
mind-reading and predictions, sensational in themselves, were
enhanced by a personality that came across forcefully on television.

A performer whose reputation was extremely high among
magicians, though his was not a household name, was the Canadian
Dai Vernon (1894–1992). Exceptionally gifted at card magic, his
forte was close-up work, though in his hands the Linking Rings
became a definitive routine which has become the basis for many
subsequent performers' sequences. Harry Jansen (1892–1955), of
Danish origin, who assisted Thurston, came to fame in his own right
as Dante and performed a number of striking illusions culminating
in the whole company being transformed into water fountains.

Since the Second World War there have been many prominent
American magicians. Originally from Germany, Siegfried and Roy
(Siegfried Fischbacher and Roy Horn) settled in Las Vegas, where
they have created an innovative modern magic spectacle. Rare
animals such as the Siberian white tiger have featured prominently
in their act; Siegfried and Roy have also made a name as
conservationists of such species. Among solo performers, David
Copperfield has achieved global fame through memorable acts
broadcast on television, including vanishing the Statue of Liberty
and walking through the Great Wall of China, and through his live
performances, which have included a horrifying sawing-through
with a circular saw and, possibly a realisation of everyone's fantasy,
flying without any visible support. Very different is the large-scale
performer John Calvert (born 1911), who has travelled the world
and survived many adventures including shipwreck and a plane
crash. He presents a varied programme ranging from hypnotism to
floating a lady seated at an organ over the heads of the audience. His
production of cigarettes from the air is astonishing. Perhaps the
greatest illusionists, who recreate some of the more artistic
presentations of the past while also performing twenty-first-century
magic with vigour and athleticism, are Jonathan and Charlotte
Pendragon. Lance Burton has a stage act which includes elegant
manipulations with doves, cards and candles, but the greatest of
such performers was Channing Pollock, who retired in his early
forties but for many magicians was the finest creator of 'sheer magic'
in modern times. Mention must also be made of the Canadian Doug
Henning (1947–2000), who brought both modernity of dress (T-
shirt and jeans) and a sense of wonder to his stage presentations.

A few names from many great European magicians may be picked
out. A brilliant early inventor was Buatier de Kolta (1847–1903),
who created a number of effects that have become classics, such as
the multiplying billiard balls. Among the illusions he originated that

Above left: *Buatier de Kolta, a brilliant and original inventor from the late-Victorian period.*
Above right: Horace *Goldin, whirlwind stage performer between c.1900 and the Second World War.*

are remarkable for their imaginative conception as well as their skilful execution are the expansion of a 6 inch (15 cm) die to a large one from which his wife appeared, and the Cocoon, in which a sketch of a silkworm leads to the appearance of a bright silk cocoon from which a woman bursts forth dressed as a butterfly. Not only did he vanish a birdcage but also, as a separate effect, a woman dressed as a bird inside a large parrot cage (both assistant and cage disappeared). Of Polish origin, Horace Goldin (1873–1939) performed at breakneck speed, while the Italian Tony Slydini moved to the United States and became best known for incredible close-up sleight-of-hand with eloquent Latin gestures. Servais Le Roy (1865–1953) from Belgium also crossed the Atlantic to create and perform a number of ingenious illusions, and also to sell magic. Kalanag (Helmut Schreiber, 1893–1963) was Germany's most famous illusionist, and toured with an action-packed evening show, including a vanishing car.

Since the Second World War magic in Europe has flourished. A 'Dutch school' of elegant manipulators produced Richard

Francis White (left), the former President of The Magic Circle, congratulates Tony Slydini, an expert close-up performer.

A 1937 programme of The Great Levante, the Australian stage performer.

Ross, with a beautiful and artistic Linking Rings routine and the barehanded production of large clocks, and above all Fred Kaps (1926–80), tall, charming and a flawless technician. From France the zany Gaetan Bloom and Dominique Duvivier have achieved fame, while in Germany modern-thinking performers such as Topas have emerged.

Distinguished performers from various other parts of the globe would have to include Aldo Richiardi (1923–85), a Peruvian, whose illusions were enhanced by dramatic yet graceful mime and gesturing; the 'Okito' dynasty (actually the Bambergs from Holland), who performed colourful oriental effects; The Great Levante (1892–1978) from Australia, with a full-length show; and Shimada from Japan, whose spectacular stagework includes fire and wrestling with an enormous dragon.

In Britain, the greatest name in magic is that of David Devant (1868–1941). For charm and geniality of character and for consummate skill at whatever he chose to perform, Devant has never been surpassed. He was master of situation comedy, producing endless eggs from a hat and piling them up in a child's arms, as well as artistic illusions such

David Devant, the greatest of British magicians.

Charles Bertram, a society entertainer of the Victorian and Edwardian eras.

as the Artist's Dream, in which a painting comes to life. He entranced audiences until about 1920, when he was affected by a form of paralysis. He is remembered for his great partnership with John Nevil Maskelyne at St George's Hall, London. A contemporary of Devant was the society entertainer Charles Bertram (1853–1907), who bore an uncanny resemblance to Edward VII. He traded on this, and indeed was an acquaintance of the King for twenty years.

A fine inventor, Percy Thomas Tibbles (1881–1938) reversed his name and achieved fame as PT Selbit. His Magic Bricks, a series of numbered blocks which rearrange themselves in any desired order, is a classic today, and his Sawing Through a Woman has been copied over and over again. In his Wrestling Cheese, a large disc of cheese resisted the strongest man's attempt to lay it flat on the stage, and the Elastic Girl stretched the unfortunate assistant's limbs in diagonal and opposing directions. The Maids of the Mist was a stunning mystery, where a simple open cabinet produced not one but five beauty queens who then vanished simultaneously and instantaneously.

A contemporary of Selbit's was Lewis Davenport (1881–1961). His act combined superb manipulation with thimbles and full-size billiard balls with bigger effects such as de Kolta's expanding die and his own Mutilated Parasol and colour-changing waistcoat. He was the founder of the Davenport dynasty which has run a magic business ever since, and his act has been partially recreated by his great-grandson Roy.

Below left: *Lewis Davenport, a skilled manipulator with full-size billiard balls.*

Roy Davenport, great-grandson of Lewis, who has recreated his great-grandfather's act, in a similar pose.

Week commencing Monday, Oct. 5th, 1942
Nightly at 7.   Matinees Thurs. & Sat., 2.30

THE GREAT LYLE
and his CAVALCADE OF MYSTERY.

1—THE KINGS THEATRE ORCHESTRA
　　　　　Under the direction of CHAS. H. PETERS
2—JOHN TILLER'S HAPPIDROME GIRLS
3—STETSON   ...   ...   "The Mad Hatter"
4—THE GREAT LYLE with Lucille Lafarge and Company
　　Magical Milliner—Flying Gramophone—Magic Chocolates—Evolution of Fashion—
　　An Indian Fable—Regal Rising.
　　HORACE GOLDIN'S THRILLER—"SAWING A WOMAN IN HALF" as recently
　　Broadcast on the Forces Programme. The girl who has been sawn in half 4,500
　　times, LILYAN DICKINSON.
　　The Cunning Bunny and FIND THE LADY (the old Racecourse Swindle as a
　　Magician sees it). Positively the most amazing illusion ever conceived. A challenge
　　to your wits !
　　THE QUEEN OF HEARTS—LUCILLE LEFARGE.
　　　　　　　　　INTERVAL
5—THE GIRLS
6—VALMAR TRIO   ...   ...   "Beauty and Grace"
7—GEORGE BOLTON   ...   ...   The Popular Gagster
8—LYLE'S "CAVALCADE OF MYSTERY"
　　A night in the Palace of Pekin—The Mandarin's Pagoda, Sands of Pekin—Chinese
　　Rice Magic—Oriental Paper Art—The Crystal Clock (Big Ben outdone).
　　WALKING THROUGH A SHEET OF GLASS (Can you see through it ?).
　　The Elusive Egg.
　　A Knotty Problem by LUCILLE LAFARGE.
　　LYLE'S Marvellous Hands. Lyle's Hands are insured for £10,000.
　　Costumes of all Nations. (The International Girl, Jose Leigh).
　　LYLE'S GREATEST MASTERPIECE : "BRIDE OF THE AIR" (she floats in the
　　air and shrivels away in full view).
　　" It all ends in smoke "—how to enjoy your smoke free of cost.
　　GUARDING THE CROWN (specially invented for LYLE by the late David Devant)
　　　　　　　　LYLE, LUCILLE LAFARGE and FULL COMPANY
　　　　　The above Programme is subject to alteration.

Next Week at 7.0,
Matinees Thursday & Saturday, 2.30,

JACK HYLTON presents

ELSIE CARLISLE AND EDDIE GRAY
in a Mirthful, Melodious Mixture

"Madames et Monsewers"

The Great Carmo, an illusionist on a grand scale, who worked with virtually a zoo of large animals.

Left: *A 1942 programme for Cecil Lyle's Cavalcade of Mystery.*

Below: *Cecil Lyle, best-known for his Magical Milliner act, with his assistant, Lucille Lafarge.*

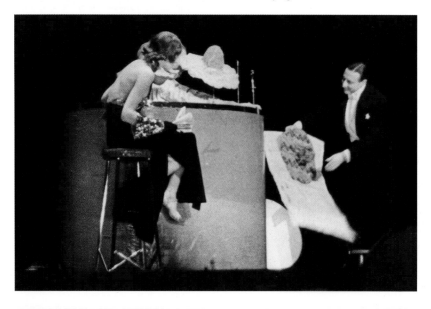

Edward Victor, a sleight-of-hand performer of exceptional skill, displays some of the objects used in his programmes.

The Great Lyle (Cecil Lyle) achieved fame through his Magical Milliner act, revolving chiefly round the production of hats, hat boxes and young ladies therefrom, while Carmo (Harry Cameron, 1881–1944) had a show which for spectacle and livestock rivalled the greats from the United States, including effects with lions, tigers and an elephant. A beautiful cut and restored necklace, known as Carmo's Beads, is still sold and performed today. Another contemporary was Edward Victor (1887–1964), whose long fingers created miracles of sleight-of-hand though he was generally booked for his hand shadows.

Oswald Williams was a great inventor though some found his performing persona arrogant. His apparatus was acquired by the Davenports, and included the production of cut-out animals from an ark and the Dizzy Limit, where an assistant in a net doubled like a hammock disappears in mid-air. A greater inventor still was Robert Harbin (1909–78), who was born in South Africa and changed his name from Ned Williams partly to avoid confusion with Oswald. He was responsible for many fine illusions, best known of which is the Zig-Zag Girl, where a girl's middle section is pushed out, unbelievably, to one side.

Below: *Oswald Williams, an English magician of the first half of the twentieth century, conducts the Substitution Trunk mystery, where an impossible exchange of two people takes place in the trunk.*

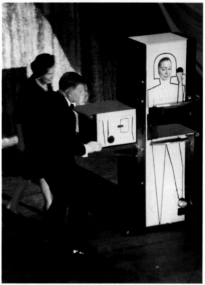

Above: *Robert Harbin during a performance of his most famous illusion, the Zig-Zag Girl, pulling the assistant's middle section out to one side.*

Above left: *Paul Daniels has the tables turned on him as his wife, Debbie McGee, subjects him to the Head Twister.*

Above right: *Arnold de Biere, a popular performer before the Second World War, famed for his Thumb Tie and Egg Bag presentations.*

Since the Second World War magic in Britain has been dominated by a small number of names. Illustrating yet again the importance of personality, Tommy Cooper (1921–84) had only to walk on stage to have his audience helpless with laughter. His gormless, well-meaning yet incompetent magician was a masterpiece of comic projection. At the same period David Nixon (1919–78) charmed television audiences with his gracious, avuncular manner, while David Berglas forged a formidable reputation for performing incredible feats of mental magic, though he was probably better known to continental television audiences than in Britain. From 1980 Paul Daniels was the best-known magical entertainer, with an act and a personality honed by hard apprenticeship in working-men's clubs. He has performed a vast array of material over many series, but in the theatre tends to concentrate on a few well-tried routines, such as the Electric Chairs, the Chop Cup with a cup and a ball, and the banknote found inside a walnut, which itself was inside an egg that was inside a lemon. Wayne Dobson looked as if he would achieve high status as a television magician but tragically was stricken with multiple sclerosis, despite which he has continued to perform live. Among today's magicians, Geoffrey Durham is perhaps the best known, a warm, affable performer whose magic is faultless and beautifully timed.

Carlton, the 'Human Hairpin', who added to his tall thin appearance with an artificial dome.

Magical apparatus

The magician has usually required equipment of some sort: until the twentieth century no one could perform a whole act by sleight-of-hand. Such props, dating from the ancient Cups and Balls onwards, may sometimes be more than they seem. Some pieces of apparatus may be marvels of mechanical ingenuity, doing much of the magician's work for him. Since the early nineteenth century apparatus has been produced to appeal as much to the amateur and hobbyist as to the professional performer – the earliest mention of the 'box of tricks' intended primarily for children is found in a German catalogue of 1803.

The 'classics of magic' generally involve apparatus. The Cups and Balls normally consist of three metal cups and small balls, which appear, vanish, transpose and eventually give way to the appearance of larger balls or possibly fruit beneath the cups. The Chinese Rings are large metal rings up to 38 cm (15 inches) in diameter that link and unlink apparently inexplicably; the number of rings used in such routines varies from two to twelve. The Egg Bag lends itself to comedy – an egg supposedly vanishes from a small cloth bag, repeatedly shown empty, but then reappears therein or sometimes changes to a glass of whisky. The Drawer Box is a wooden box with an empty sliding drawer that becomes filled with whatever the

The Cups and Balls used by Prince Charles at The Magic Circle in 1975.

An inlaid drawer box of the nineteenth century.

A card box of the nineteenth century, for producing or vanishing a card.

The Card Pedestal, for making a card appear or disappear.

performer chooses. Some of the famous effects of card magic may require no more than a pack of cards, but some large-scale versions of Find the Lady, for example, call for specially made large cards and perhaps a stand to display them.

During the Victorian era the production and selling of magical apparatus expanded dramatically. There were specialised magic dealers, who sold equipment, often made in their own workshops, and issued catalogues, the early examples of which are very scarce and in great demand by collectors. The 'box of tricks' was well established by 1830 and the contents were already so standardised that they are similar to many twentieth-century sets. At that early date several items were turned in wood; later tin or other metal gradually came in as suitable materials for tubes or gimmicks of various kinds.

Small alarm clocks for production from a hat.

Above left: *The Crystal Casket, for producing silk handkerchiefs, or, as illustrated, a large ball.*
Above right: *The 'Fairy Box for Florins' of the nineteenth century, for making coins disappear singly.*

A stick used by Chung Ling Soo for making a handkerchief vanish.

Left: *A decorated tole funnel for comic effect, involving producing milk or water from a spectator's elbow.*

Right: *An appearing rose-tree (!) of the nineteenth century.*

*A vase made in sterling silver, c.1850, used by
John Henry Anderson, the 'Wizard of the North'.*

Several items were common from the earliest times. The ball and egg vases were turned containers on stems that would permit a ball or egg to appear, vanish or reappear. The 'Grandmother's Necklace' originally comprised three large wooden beads that were released from string tied through and round them. The Obedient Ball was a wooden ball, threaded on a cord, which would slide down and stop on command. Pillars for cut and restored string were also frequently found, as were various paper and card items.

Some Victorian apparatus aspired to a degree of elegance, particularly those items made of wood. Drawer boxes and caskets might be inlaid, and the term 'treen' was sometimes used in reference to small wooden articles such as cups. Tinware was often japanned, or varnished with a black lacquer, and might be painted decoratively; such items were referred to as toleware. Apparatus was made to be attractive and prestigious in its own right: John Henry Anderson, the Wizard of the North, performed with sterling silver

*A display of turned
wooden objects, or treen,
from the nineteenth
century.*

A nineteenth-century drawer box, made by Professor Norris, for producing various items.

equipment, some of which is in the possession of The Magic Circle. Professor Norris, a mid-Victorian magician, had his workshop next to his theatre and used to rush from one to the other, flinging on his costume over his working clothes. He produced apparatus for sale in wood and metal, including a large ornate ball vase.

The nineteenth century was the heyday of the cluttered table, laden with boxes, bottles, stands and all sorts of

Above: *A large nineteenth-century ornate Ball Vase, made by Professor Norris.*

A nineteenth-century metal swan, made by Professor Norris. The swan picks out a chosen playing card.

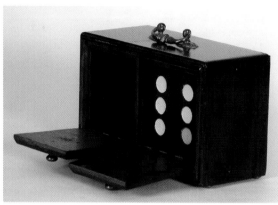

A Die Box, a classic children's effect involving the adventures of a large wooden die.

A Clock Dial, probably from the early twentieth century. The hand is spun and stops at any chosen hour.

Right: A Card-Go, a wooden frame by Jack Hughes for the disappearance of a card.

Left: A Coffee Vase, probably from the early twentieth century. Hot coffee is produced from a vase which has first been shown empty and then filled with cotton wool.

Right: A padlock made by John Martin, an expert craftsman in metal.

Left: *A barrel, as used by Claudine in the 1950s and 1960s, for the production of a dog.*

Above left: *A Coin Pail made by Ross Bertram for the 'Miser's Dream' production of coins from the air.*

Above: *A Scroll and Balls, as performed by the comedy magician Billy McComb.*

Left: *A flowering rosebush, as used by the Pendragons and made by John Gaughan, a highly skilled American craftsman.*

Below: *The billiard balls used by Paula Baird in her manipulative act, and the wand presented to her by The Magic Circle.*

A decorative tole cone attached to a gun for vanishing a handkerchief.

paraphernalia. Although performers later used less equipment, magical dealers and their wares proliferated, mainly to satisfy the demands of the rising numbers of amateurs. Initially apparatus was entirely hand-made by craftsmen in workshops but with the advent of mass-production technology and, eventually, cheap materials such as plastic, more and more was produced in factories.

In some ways magic is a conservative art, though in others, particularly methods and presentation, it can be progressive and groundbreaking. The magic routines that have become classics use apparatus that has hardly changed over more than a century. Materials may have changed, but the appearance remains the same. Likewise, the accessories that a magician tends to use most – rope, cards, silk handkerchiefs, coins, dice – have also stayed the same.

Left: *Apparatus sold by Blands in the nineteenth century, for producing or exchanging items.*

A bag on a long handle used by David Devant, for exchanging items dropped in by the audience.

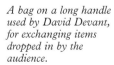

Dealers and makers

The main centres for the manufacture of magical equipment in the nineteenth century were France, Germany, the United States and Britain. Germany was particularly known for fine and intricate metalwork, and in neighbouring Austria the firm of Klingl from 1876 produced apparatus that is highly prized today. In the United States Burlingame (established 1872) and Martinka (Germany 1860, USA 1873) led the way.

Despite the modern trend of producing items in bulk quantity, there has always been room for the specialist and expert craftsman. From the time of Robert-Houdin, who started his career as a maker of clocks and watches and subsequently turned his expertise to magical purposes, there have been highly regarded manufacturers either of individual items for use in a particular show (sometimes the performer was his own craftsman) or for more general use via dealers. In the United States Floyd Thayer, an expert wood-turner, produced high-quality apparatus in wood and then formed his own company to sell the products. Two of Thayer's best workmen, the Owen Brothers, set up their own independent operation. At the same time, Carl Brema produced precision-made brass items, while the Petrie-Lewis Manufacturing Company made high-quality equipment, especially in metal, for fifty years. In Germany fine metalwork came from Carl Willmann in the late nineteenth century and the firms of Conradi and Bartl in the twentieth. In Britain John Martin, another watchmaker, created precision items in metal and accessories for individual clients in the 1940s, and George Hammerton produced metal items such as Card Swords, Multiplying Candles and Card Appearing in Balloon stands until around 1970.

140   G. ORNUM & Co., 4, Duke Street, Charing Cross, London.

1563 The Fairy Casket, Die and Handkerchief. — A very handsome casket, beautifully polished in ebony and inlaid is freely shown, also a solid die, which is placed into the casket, just filling it, after which the casket is locked. A borrowed handkerchief is now made to disappear, and is discovered in the casket instead of the die, which has disappeared in a borrowed hat. The die is now made to disappear and passes back into the casket, while the borrowed handkerchief is discovered in the hat. A beautiful combination trick.

Price complete 20/-, post-free 20/6.

1564 The Perfected Disappearing Christmas Tree. — The performer presents in an ordinary flower pot a Christmas tree 14-ins. high, covered with presents, bon-bons, etc., and 1½ lighted candles. The presents are distributed amongst the juvenile portion of the audience, and then the performer stating that nothing is left now but the tree and the lighted candles, asks who will have the lot, so saying he throws the tree and lighted candles towards the audience, but the whole lot disappears like a flash of lightning, and nothing remains. A most startling termination of the trick, and easy to perform.

Price 21/-, post-free 21/6.

1565 The Tray, Die, Handkerchief and Cage. — A live bird in cage is shown, covered by the handkerchief, and given to a spectator to hold. The solid die is placed on the tray, and given to another spectator to hold. A hat is now borrowed, shown empty, and placed on a chair. The conjurer now commands the articles to change places, shakes the handkerchief to prove the cage has disappeared. In place of the die out flies the bird, whilst on looking into the hat the solid die is found therein. A most effective combination, and easily worked.

Price 24/-, post-free 25/-.

Full directions sent with each Article

A page from an Ornum & Company catalogue of the 1900s (proprietor George Munro).

A Nest of Boxes, as sold by Davenports in the 1950s. A borrowed ring disappears and is found in the innermost of the boxes.

Right: *A Dove Pan, as sold by Davenports in the 1950s. An empty pan is filled with incongruous ingredients, and a live dove or cake appears in their place.*

The Demon Wonder Box was of German origin but was made famous by Davenports. An innocent-looking silver box produces a number of silk handkerchiefs.

In London the most remarkable and long-lasting dealer is the family firm of Davenports, established in 1898. The founder, Lewis Davenport, was a performer who first sold magic as a supplementary means of income but concentrated on it when his performing days were over. When his sons, known as Gus and Gilly, took over, the business bought out other dealers' businesses, such as Will Goldston's, and collections. It is possible, even today, to purchase items dating from the 1930s, often originating in Germany, which have by now acquired antique status. Lewis's granddaughter Betty is in charge, with her husband Fergus Roy, and their sons are actively involved to secure the future of the dynasty. Established sellers of

A page from Gamages catalogue, 'Gamagic', 1937.

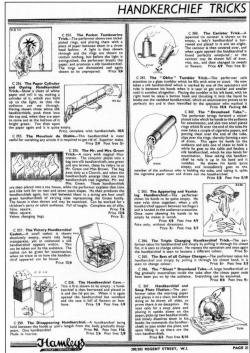

A page from Hamleys magic catalogue, 1934.

The Ink Change trick, advertised in Servais Le Roy's 'Magical Monthly', June 1913.

magic have often been associated with famous London stores. Hamleys in Regent Street have had a magic department since they took over Blands of Oxford Street (the earliest London magical dealer) in the late nineteenth century, and Gamages, a large general store, had one for many years till it closed in about 1970. Ellisdons, too, was a department store with a prominent magic section, which closed a few years earlier. However, to magicians the specialist magic store has always had its own strong appeal, providing a focal point where visiting performers can meet. Among many such shops in London Will Goldston's (till 1946), Harry Stanley's Unique Magic Studio (till 1971), Ken Brooke's Magic Place and the International Magic Studio, which is still in business, are all worthy of mention.

Dealers do not necessarily have to have a large shop. Many work by mail-order, and some, like the Supreme Magic Company, run from 1954 to 1987 by the energetic Edwin Hooper, did extremely good business this way and probably had a larger range of wares than any other dealer. Besides their postal business, the main outlets for such dealers are conventions and gatherings of various sorts (the British Ring Convention accommodates up to sixty dealers or more

A page from an export catalogue of Conradi-Horster, Berlin, c.1920s.

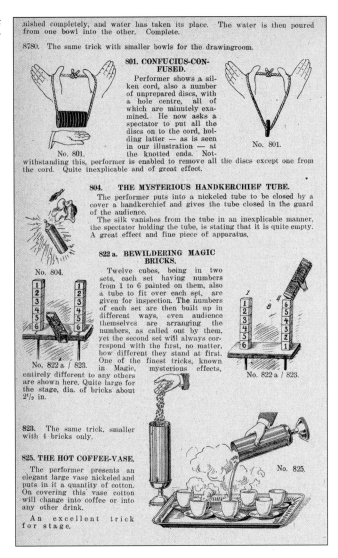

...nished completely, and water has taken its place. The water is then poured from one bowl into the other. Complete.

8780. The same trick with smaller bowls for the drawingroom.

801. CONFUCIUS-CON-FUSED.

Performer shows a silken cord, also a number of unprepared discs, with a hole centre, all of which are minutely examined. He now asks a spectator to put all the discs on to the cord, holding latter — as is seen in our illustration — at the knotted ends. Notwithstanding this, performer is enabled to remove all the discs except one from the cord. Quite inexplicable and of great effect.

No. 801.

No. 801.

804. THE MYSTERIOUS HANDKERCHIEF TUBE.

The performer puts into a nickeled tube to be closed by a cover a handkerchief and gives the tube closed in the guard of the audience.

The silk vanishes from the tube in an inexplicable manner, the spectator holding the tube, is stating that it is quite empty. A great effect and fine piece of apparatus.

No. 804.

822 a. BEWILDERING MAGIC BRICKS.

Twelve cubes, being in two sets, each set having numbers from 1 to 6 painted on them, also a tube to fit over each set, are given for inspection. The numbers of each set are then built up in different ways, even audience themselves are arranging the numbers, as called out by them, yet the second set will always correspond with the first, no matter, how different they stand at first. One of the finest tricks, known in Magic, mysterious effects,

No. 822 a / 823. entirely different to any others are shown here. Quite large for the stage, dia. of bricks about 2¹/₂ in.

No. 822 a / 823.

823. The same trick, smaller with 4 bricks only.

825. THE HOT COFFEE-VASE.

The performer presents an elegant large vase nickeled and puts in it a quantity of cotton. On covering this vase cotton will change into coffee or into any other drink.

An excellent trick for stage.

No. 825.

from around the world), as well as demonstrations to the many magical societies around Britain.

Catalogues are an important part of the business of magic dealers. These have varied tremendously in scope, size and presentation, according to the range of the dealer's wares and the era in which the catalogue was produced. Illustrations can vary from engravings to linework and photographs, and the aim is always for optimum appeal, sometimes resulting in the reader being considerably misled. The 'rose tree' offered in one Victorian catalogue turns out to be a full 4 cm (just over an inch and a half) high! Everything must appear

Tambourine Rings. Usually a huge coil of paper or satin ribbon is produced from the two rings, clamped over a single sheet of paper.

Right: *Glitter balls and a rhinestone-studded thimble as used by manipulators.*

to be a miracle, and descriptions are worded accordingly. Dealers might well include goods from abroad, and there were tie-ups between, for example, some English dealers such as Davenports and their German counterparts between the world wars. Today it is possible to obtain almost anything from the United States, Japan or Europe through a British dealer. Furthermore, some catalogues are now published on the Internet or on CD-ROMs, permitting the use of more colour in the illustrations.

The Chinese Sticks, made by George Kovari. Two cords with tassels passing through the ends of bamboo sticks lengthen and shorten mysteriously.

Magic posters

One of the most appealing and attractive elements of magical history is the poster. These have varied enormously, from plain text announcing a forthcoming performance to portraits and elaborate scenes depicting (or purporting to depict) a miracle from the magician's show. The quality of the artwork can likewise vary considerably, but there is no doubt that at their best posters can reflect the very best of graphic art. The purpose is, of course, advertising, and that can often mean reality is embellished in order to create a greater expectation of the marvels to be witnessed. Some posters concentrate on personality, portraying the performer in a suitably mysterious light, while others focus on an illusion or other effect to be performed, sometimes by means of a series of vignettes showing the progressive stages of the effect.

John Henry Anderson ushered in the age of the magic poster at the beginning of Queen Victoria's reign. Posters are still being produced today, though probably the most artistic pre-date the Second World War. Techniques have changed over the years as the technology of printing generally has developed. The stone lithography of the nineteenth and early twentieth centuries has given way to the photography and scanning of the digital age. The colouring of the stone lithos can be, however, especially subtle and pleasing. Very large posters could be printed in 'sheets' (sections).

Early posters were often intended to heighten expectation and to play on people's credulity by emphasising the supernatural (though usually in a humorous way). Imps, goblins and demons appeared as a sort of supporting cast in a poster, as in the case of the great

A poster for the 'Comedians de Mephisto', Servais Le Roy and his assistants, Talma, an accomplished sleight-of-hand magician in her own right, and Bosco, a comic stooge.

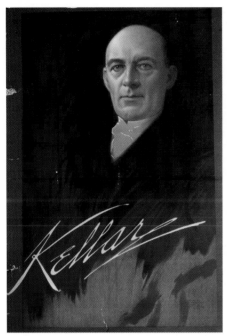

A poster of the famous American magician Harry Kellar.

American magicians Herrmann, Kellar and Thurston, while Houdini had a hideous devil-like monster pressing down on his Water Torture Cell escape. A sense of otherworldly mystery also pervades such images as that of the lady magician Ionia, who presented an exotic act of eastern-style magic.

In Britain the most memorable posters fittingly commemorate David Devant. The emphasis is on more human qualities – 'all done by kindness' – especially in those by the artist John Hassall. Will Owen, a follower of Hassall, also depicted Devant, introducing a demon rather incongruously to illustrate the Vanishing Motorcycle and Rider.

The most sought-after posters are those portraying Chung Ling Soo. They all try to engender a feeling of oriental mystery, of the unknown and exotic world of the East, where

Below: *A poster of David Devant.*

Below: *A poster for Chung Ling Soo and 'The Land of the Peacock', suggestive of exotic Eastern mysteries.*

A poster depicting Chung Ling Soo as an artist with his palette (right), and (above) the original artwork for the poster.

Two posters of Chung Ling Soo. (Above) The Birth of a Pearl, his famous illusion of the appearance of a young lady from a shell. (Right) The magician depicted as if behind a bead curtain.

Above: *Two posters depicting Chung Ling Soo: (left) blowing smoke towards a covered vase which will fill with the smoke; (right) producing a butterfly woman.*

miracles undreamed of in Western acts might be created. Soo himself is sometimes shown lost in an enigmatic reverie, not letting us in on what he is thinking but leaving us to surmise that he is no doubt pondering some new piece of enchantment. In other posters he is caught in a performance of his famous repertoire, or there is symbolism – the palette and brushes equating Soo's art with that of the painter, for example. Many of the posters were produced in England despite Soo's being an American.

Modern posters contain realism (with the use of photographs) or contemporary design. The approach has clearly changed: it is no longer appropriate to suggest diabolical forces at work, nor is it necessary to produce a great work of art. The modern poster is functional: it needs to be striking and have immediate impact.

A poster of the magician Ionia, who performed an act inspired by Egypt and the oriental, c.1910.

Magicians' societies

Clubs or societies for magicians have flourished since the beginning of the twentieth century. As with any hobby, interest or profession, it is natural for those of a like mind to wish to come together and create an organisation for social purposes, to share knowledge and to promote their particular interest. In the case of magic, societies have from the start embraced both amateurs and professionals. The oldest organisations are the Society of Detroit Magicians (1894) and the Society of American Magicians, founded in 1902 on the suggestion of two New York amateurs, the purpose being 'to promote harmony among those interested in Magic, and to further the elevation of the Art'. In Britain two major societies were established in 1905, the British Magical Society, based in Birmingham, and a few months later The Magic Circle, London. The Mahatma Magic Circle, based in Liverpool, also has an early origin.

Since that time many societies have sprung up all over the world, some with more success than others. Of these the International Brotherhood of Magicians has from its inception in the USA in the 1920s grown steadily to become the largest in the world. The British arm ('Ring') of the IBM holds an annual convention and attracts up to fifteen hundred registrants from many countries for five days of shows, lectures, dealer displays and other events. The largest international magical gathering, however, is the triennial Congress of the Fédération Internationale des Sociétés Magiques (FISM), held in various capital cities. In Britain the society scene is very active and energetic, encompassing in 2004 over one hundred recognised clubs. Anyone interested in magic can approach these societies: membership is often granted after an audition. Some societies have youth sections, intended to encourage and develop budding magicians.

David Berglas (right), an outstandingly original thinker and performer, with Professor Edwin Dawes, leading magical historian.

Fred Kaps (left), an international magic prizewinner, and Lewis Ganson, one of the greatest authors of books for magicians.

Of special interest is The Magic Circle, in popular opinion the definitive magical organisation. In its initial circulation to more than fifteen hundred magicians, the letter of invitation stated that the Circle was set up 'to form the nucleus of a vast congress of magicians of all nationalities, striving to elevate and purify the art, and raise it to one of the first professions'. Its purpose was also to prevent public exposure of magical secrets, a perennial problem, and hence the motto of the new society, *Indocilis privata loqui* – 'Unwilling to speak of private things'. The society has a hierarchy of degrees, rising to Member of the Inner Magic Circle. It is said that the initials of The Magic Circle were to commemorate the lately deceased Martin Chapender, a brilliant performer who died tragically young.

From the earliest times The Magic Circle sought its own permanent headquarters. After taking up temporary residence in a number of hotels and other premises, the ambition was finally realised in 1998, with the opening of its own building with freehold in Stephenson Way, near Euston, London. This accommodates a theatre, clubrooms, a library and a museum, and is a Mecca for magicians from all over the world. The Circle's programme is, as it always has been, a mixture of lectures, performances and related events, some for magicians and some for the public. The official body controlling the property is the Centre for the Magic Arts Ltd, responsible in particular for corporate hire and with a wider general brief to educate the public in the art and history of magic.

Chris Charlton, an English performer of the mid twentieth century, passes milk through the body of his assistant.

Further reading

General histories of magic

Christopher, Milbourne. *Panorama of Magic*. Dover, New York, 1962.
Christopher, Milbourne. *The Illustrated History of Magic*. Thomas Crowell, New York, 1973.
Dawes, Edwin A. *The Great Illusionists*. David & Charles, 1979.
Doerflinger, William. *The Magic Catalogue*. Dutton, New York, 1977.
Fisher, John. *Paul Daniels and the Story of Magic*. Jonathan Cape, 1987.
Reynolds, Charles and Regina. *100 Years of Magic Posters*. Hart-Davis/MacGibbon, 1976.

Individual performers

Cramer, Stuart. *Germain the Wizard*. The Miracle Factory, Seattle, 2002.
Dawes, Edwin A. *Charles Bertram: the Court Conjurer*. Kaufman & Company, Washington DC, 1997.
Dawes, Edwin A. *Stanley Collins: Conjurer, Collector and Iconoclast*. Kaufman & Company, Washington DC, 2002.
Gibson, Walter B. *The Original Houdini Scrapbook*. Sterling Publishing Company, New York, 1976.
Karr, Todd (compiler). *The Silence of Chung Ling Soo*. The Miracle Factory, Seattle, 2001.
Lewis, Eric C., and Warlock, Peter. *PT Selbit: Magical Innovator*. Magical Publications, Pasadena, 1989.
Sharpe, S. H. *Devant's Delightful Delusions*. Magical Publications, Pasadena, 1990.
Waldron, Daniel. *Blackstone: a Magician's Life*. Meyerbooks, Glenwood, Illinois, 1999.
Warlock, Peter. *Buatier de Kolta: Genius of Illusion*. Magical Publications, Pasadena, 1993.
Wraxall, Lascelles (translator). *Memoirs of Robert-Houdin, King of the Conjurers*. Dover, New York, 1964.

The museum and premises of The Magic Circle are open to the public on certain occasions throughout the year, in particular the 'Meet The Magic Circle' evenings. For details of these, contact the organiser: Diane O'Brien, 82 Windsor Drive, Dartford, Kent DA1 3HN. Telephone: 01322 221592.

The Magic Circle headquarters is at 12 Stephenson Way, London NW1 2HD. Telephone enquiries: 020 7387 2222. Website: www.themagiccircle.co.uk

Davenports can be found at 5, 6 & 7 Charing Cross Underground Arcade, The Strand, London WC2N 4HZ. Telephone: 020 7836 0408. Website: www.davenportsmagic.co.uk

David Blaine started as a street magician in the United States but has progressed to more sensational stunts, such as his feat of endurance surviving in a box suspended near Tower Bridge, London, for forty-four days in 2003.

Index of names

Please note that many of the names below are stage names: real names are given in brackets only when they have appeared in the main text.

Anderson, John Henry 5, 10, 22, 33
Baird, Paula 25
Bamberg family 14
Bartl 27
Berglas, David 18, 37
Bertram, Charles 15
Bertram, Ross 25
Blackstone, Harry (Junior) 11
Blackstone, Harry (Senior) 11
Blaine, David 39
Blands 26, 30
Bloom, Gaetan 14
Bosco 33
Brema, Carl 27
British Magical Society 37
British Ring (International Brotherhood of Magicians) 30, 37
Brooke, Ken 30
Brunel, Isambard Kingdom 5
Burlingame 27
Burton, Lance 12
Calvert, John 12
Cardini (Richard Pitchford) 11
Carlton 18
Carmo 16
Carroll, Lewis 5
Centre for the Magic Arts Ltd 38
Chapender, Martin 38
Charles, HRH Prince 2, 19
Charlton, Chris 38
Chefalo 8
Cheops, King 4
Ching Ling Foo 9
Chung Ling Soo (William Ellsworth Robinson) 1, 9, 21, 34, 35, 36
Claudine 25
Conradi 27, 31
Cooke, George 4
Cooper, Tommy 18
Copperfield, David 12
Daniels, Paul 18
Dante (Harry Jansen) 12
Davenport, Betty 28
Davenport, Gilly 28
Davenport, Gus 28
Davenport, Lewis 15

Davenport, Roy 15
Davenports 28, 32, 39
Dawes, Edwin 37
de Biere, Arnold 18
de Kolta, Buatier 12, 15
Dedi 4
Devant, David 4, 5, 14, 15, 26, 34
Dickens, Charles 5
Disraeli, Benjamin 5
Dobson, Wayne 18
Downs, T. Nelson 6
Dunninger, Joseph 12
Durham, Geoffrey 18
Duvivier, Dominique 14
Egyptian Hall 4
Ellisdons 30
Fédération Internationale des Sociétés Magiques (FISM) 37
Gamages 29
Ganson, Lewis 38
Gaughan, John 25
Germain, Karl 11
Gilbert, William Schwenck 4, 5
Goldin, Horace 3, 13
Goldston, Will 28, 30
Hamleys 29, 30
Hammerton, George 27
Harbin, Robert (Ned Williams) 17
Hassall, John 34
Henning, Doug 12
Herrmann, Adelaide 9
Herrmann, Alexander 9, 34
Hofzinser, Johann 9
Hooper, Edwin 30
Houdin, Robert 5, 10
Houdini, Harry 6, 10, 11
Hughes, Jack 24
International Brotherhood of Magicians 37
International Magic Studio 30
Ionia 2, 36
Kalanag (Helmut Schreiber) 13
Kaps, Fred 14, 38
Kellar, Harry 9, 10, 34
Klingl 27
Kovari, George 32
Le Roy, Servais 13, 30, 33
Levante 14

Lyle, Cecil 16, 17
Magic Circle, The 37, 38, 39
Mahatma Magic Circle 37
Martin, John 24
Martinka 27
Maskelyne, Jasper 4
Maskelyne, John Nevil 4, 15
McComb, Billy 25
McGee, Debbie 18
Murray 6, 7
Nixon, David 18
Norris, Professor 23
Ornum & Company (George Munro) 27
Owen, Will 34
Owen Brothers 27
Pendragon, Jonathan and Charlotte 12
Petrie-Lewis Manufacturing Company 27
Pollock, Channing 12
Richiardi, Aldo 14
Ross, Richard 14
Roy, Fergus 28
Selbit, PT (Percy Thomas Tibbles) 15
Seneca 4
Shimada 14
Siegfried and Roy 12
Slydini, Tony 13
Society of American Magicians 37
Society of Detroit Magicians 37
Stanley, Harry 30
Sterling, Max 9
Stillwell, George 6
Sullivan, Arthur 4
Supreme Magic Company 30
Talma 33
Thayer, Floyd 27
Thurston, Howard 6, 10, 34
Thurston, Jane 10
Topas 14
Unique Magic Studio 30
Vernon, Dai 12
Victor, Edward 17
White, Francis 13
Williams, Oswald 17
Willmann, Carl 27
Winter, Faith 5